Rove

Laurie D Graham

[signature]

Sarah,

I hope you enjoy this
book, and I hope to see
you soon!

Oct 21/13

Library and Archives Canada Cataloguing in Publication

Graham, Laurie D, author
        Rove / Laurie D. Graham.

(Strike fire new authors series)
Poems.
ISBN 978-1-926710-23-5 (pbk.)

I. Title. II. Series: Strike fire new authors series

PS8613.R344R69 2013   C811ʾ.6   C2013-906109-6

Edited by Harold Rhenisch.
Designed and typeset by Donald Ward.
Cover photograph: "Rural Municipality of White Valley, Saskatchewan," by John Conway.
Cover Design: Tania Wolk, Go Giraffe Go.
Set in Adobe Garamond Pro.
Printed and bound in Canada.

The publishers gratefully acknowledge the assistance of the Saskatchewan Arts Board, The Canada Council for the Arts, and the Creative Industry Growth and Sustainability program, made possible through funding provided to the Saskatchewan Arts Board by the Government of Saskatchewan through the Ministry of Tourism, Parks, Culture, and Sport.

Hagios Press
Box 33024 Cathedral po
Regina sk   s4t 7x2
www.hagiospress.com

for Family

Rove

Say cloverleaf, polyethylene.
Say this parking lot slinks into marshland. Say it bristles into scrubland.

Say this mall becomes a bonfire;
you travel its plastic smoke.

Say sky, fescue, say Wîsahkêcâhk, say La Vérendrye and Henday.
Say heart-choke, say groundbreak, say garrison

with gunbarrel eyes. Say there's a fist yelling *This is my apartment now*
in a language you don't know.

Say geno-matri-patricide, regicide and terracide and skyocide,
say sapling, say childblood, cry doctor,

say your piece then get out, say translate, please, translate.
Say coyote, say smallpox, say creekbottom — look: Wîsahkêcâhk.

Say Big Bear. Say Frog Lake, fresh loam, buffalo

hide, free land, thistle, aspen, sweat.
Riel, say Riel can govern in Michif.

Say colour, say colourless eye, say Queen's portrait,
say here, here is mine, I bought it,

say settler, claim poverty, profess better and see the felled trees,
say brethren, bread and wagons; say Spanish flu,

say railyard, sing the combustion engine,
say the singing of your name in the new air,

say virgin territory and believe it.

Say the Lord's bounty, say the wheatfields, say the dust, pick the rocks,
say canola and soybean, thresh, thrush,

say the laundry on the line, say the dank root cellar,
say the numbers, tell the Wheat Board where to go,

say it fast like an auction and move to the city,
say minimum wage and grunt while you work,

say benefits and rigpig derrick oilsand tailings pond boom —
say busted skull, say tuition fund and heritage fund,

say concrete scaffold, say it far from home, say the length of your commute
at the sound of the tone, say Ralph Klein and spit in the dirt.

Say Sky Dancer, say Zwicky. Say Alberta and Saskatchewan
and switch the order. Say Wayne Gretzky Drive,

say it's five-on-three and he's on a breakaway,
scream it in the riot on Canada Day, whisper it into your lager,

say it from the hollow of the couch, say it while you piss in the alley,
hiss it into your lover's ear, say it to your broker and his secretaries,

tell it to the lawyer, to the landlord when the heat's turned off and the pipes freeze,
say it again to the food bank and again to the caseworker:

say cloverleaf highway polyethylene grocery sack.

Say fluorescent lightbulbs will save
the earth, say there's a heart

in the middle of it (Please tell me you can hear it),
say glut and Democracy, say it in absentia,

say your little heartbeat, send it through the layers,
say it in the muck in this marsh, in this bristling parking lot.

Now this family living on homesteads around Angle Lake and Meadow,
sitting around the table Saturdays before or after the dance,

cigarettes and brown beerbottles,
a family of ships run aground in the stiff grass.

Now two dogs loping the acres surrounding,
bought from the Trans Alta lineman to keep the chickens safe, and the colts.

Bullet a streak across the hard brown after the coyote.
Punch, the killer, fear-eyed and big as a horse.

Now the violent ribs of dogs drawn soft in childhood sleep
where Punch sits, Bullet sits, ears cocked at motion

along the road, posing with the others, cigarettes
and brown beerbottles, and the ability to laugh.

Say they learned Ukrainian, these English dogs
on land of *néhiyawak*,

ten bucks, a hundred-sixty acres, a gift
to my grandparents for obeying the rubric of farm.

Now, in citied sleep, the sweepers sluicing the avenue
after the music's turned off,

Punch and Bullet corralling the young ones out of the bars and back
to their capsizing suburbs.

Say one was shot,
mistaken by the neighbour for a coyote —

the other found at the shore of the lake with his chest torn away.
These dogs like ships, tracking such a great distance.

Three pencilled names on a torn page
in my mother's jewel box: *Bolishi, Moatiski, Drogowich.*

Not sure where these are
but I'm from there, in part.

Ukrainians clearing poplars from their hundred-sixty acres
all winter, vowing never to utter those names again.

The grass-green bed of the suburb in windshot
of Refinery Row. The displace of airplane, Greyhound, ship

across, house across field into town,
the men all around, hollering it to its destination.

See the house peeking through bushrows at Second Street,
two tight rooms the width of my grandfather's memory

when the house was still on the homestead,
gazing high and west and south over the swells.

Watch the twelve horses pulling it to town.
Might've been winter but probably not

and old widows can't farm homesteads alone.
See the bow of the window glass,

foundation sinking in the ebb of yard,
the oldest thing I know besides the arrowheads,

or the small gold cross in my mother's jewel box —
Baba stopping the school bus in a blizzard to clasp it around her scoured neck.

See the barn on the homestead chipping grey and collapsing
as you read this,

and the house in town, stooped under good new shingles and strong chimney.
There's nothing to say what survives.

Now conjure a boy,
nice enough and shy.

Carrying a sadness not entirely his own.
He doesn't know his father, though they sleep one room apart.

The boy grows up and has to marry, because he has to,
because that's how.

Assume the woman is too smart and she gets angry.
Farming doesn't give him nothing,

neither will the job at the hospital.
Retirement, widowerhood.

Grief.

There's his daughter working checkout at the Safeway,
taking the teaching route

instead of the nursing route because this is the Sixties and
you can do whatever you want. Her mother on the farm

wanting the nursing route but instead
given a husband:

sad, sick, about to auction off to the city —
sending the daughter off with every blessing.

The young woman able to breathe at last,
weighing bags of oranges, punching

out the numbers, bobbing
in the chop of the lecture hall.

Will her own daughter track up the highway
after some almost invisible river,

will she ferry herself east to Canadian London,
walk a field of soybeans after some desk job?

Will she stretch the length of the Straight of Juan de Fuca
twice yearly, bomb south from Edmonton —

a two-four of hours gets you Salt Lake City?
Will she reach the breadth of humanity

on a two-day Greyhound bus?
Will she have her kernel

planted, wantonly planted, in the self-same,
wouldn't-you-know-it place,

beyond need, seasickness, the story of land,
beyond this grief in wild crowns?

Were there buffalo here? Will there be crops planted?
The family round the table never talking

about what they have to do to get the land working. The Saturday
dances get told, the roving packs of musicians,

the roving doctors, the young men
on the threshing crews — *those three nice Indian brothers,*

what were their names, saying catcha mayesh
for Як ся маєш *to the women in town —*

going to church, singing Mass;
the blessed bread,

the tidied graves. Then oil is discovered and they rove away.
Two generations of farmers: the wars

fought to have this right to vacate.
See the branches of the suburbs blossom wild with bungalows.

See the grass-green, the oil refinery, the tight grey brickwork of a city
shamed to forgetfulness. Big Bear, look, these brick lanes

are the reason you were starved off. Wandering Spirit, look,
no place for a warrior but the streets and the penthouses;

this is why you were hung. Look, there's no ground here;
they've stretched the concrete flat. Look how big,

the houses in the valley, look at this religion of parking lots.
You know they plant these crops all over.

They won't tell us how much the oil wells spend —
they show the paper flying from hands and pockets.

And look how people beg on corners,
bless the rotgut whisky,

look they rove on air and water,
gazing down the blinking planet.

Look what they do to sleep inside.
And remember how the soldiers kept on coming.

Now Baba's memory of Cossacks thundering west down Whyte,
tough, bald heads and beards and stinking tunics and cocked rifles

and the hooves casting wide circles
and the horses crazed for being too much alive.

On the bus bench, staring down the Army & Navy,
chest full to bursting in the Cossack charge,

I aim my mind's rifle at the patio-dwellers,
at the citizens holding fast to their corners

relying on the light's ability to change, who turn up their imperial noses —
these Cossacks another abominable delay,

a way to show the daily ease of their anger.
And bless the trinket shops behind me, anonymous and mutable,

leaning away from their squat brick limits towards the scent of Cossacks
stirring garbage and dust,

the flying tails of matted hair, the dangerous torsos, the swords
clanging. Bless my mother remembering

Baba remembering Cossacks like a bad wind,
wild hippie howling men, gazes haunted by want and possession,

Baba frighted into stillness as a girl, not knowing what she'd do
if she lifted one foot off the dirt road

in their presence, and me not knowing if there was dirt or cement under her feet
to begin with, these Cossacks bellowing with their swords, or rifles,

aloft, crushing the pavement and the piping beneath, these dutiful,
pissed-off citizens waiting at the crosswalks for a destroyed road,

the tremors of impossible existence; one at the rear turning
on the back of his horse and pointing his sword, at me,

his rifle — at me;

a heavy laugh bumping his spine through the curvature of horse
and I swear the earth curves in concert — the furthest reaches

of Baba's old world. The quaking depth of his laugh
and he's blasting west and my foot

rises above the concrete, two inches . . . three . . .

as the last of them charges toward the moneyed halls of learning,
the museums of bone and shale — the Cossacks will destroy them —

I know this is more than a memory of a mother's memory
of a great-grandmother's memory

of a world she stepped out of so neatly in my mind
and into Canada.

See this soil swallowed in thin, hard
gulps in all the cities I've lived.

Make this street a field-edge. Look, the birthing crops
are nameless.

If it looks like foxtail, it's barley,
she said.

The wind gathering,
the dirtcrust waning, the chemical smell on the air,

the mown miles, the refinery
floating its garbage across my childhood sky;

my mother picking rocks from the sky as a child:
all the places she can go.

See it recede, this field full of crop, wisped.
Speak this epoch of weeds through concrete.

It was in the middle of
      In the name of Narid
                 the line
                         suknatskyj warm in taxi

Whole language warm in taxi!
Whole sad family in that line!

     It was in your father's *didoperepolokh*
             scaring nothing, not sparrows, not neighbour widows

   My *dido* buying first car
          pacing city yard

             in soiled farmboots
                In this accent I pronounce

       from language lobbed
                over small heads

eet vahss you
you veel pay forr dheec
        '*pohanyn*'
It was in words shipped

       to this apartment
         this eastern city

(What right do I have
     my father's people

        from Ballymena
           and Campbelltown
half right
    to tell half-story

        pohanyn
          trying to burn the church)

It was in *Wood Mountain*
         Poems: you left

                         on Greyhound
                                   aimed at mountains

                 knowing something's over
                         but still alive

You saw its flames
         lick your new bed

                             You saw it and you named it

                 It's in how you don't write

                                 a single thing
                                       suknatskyj

In the ice whispering
the bare birch,

in light a blank sheet.
In dunes of shorn crop,

ghostpasture thrumming.
In three generations

pushing silk flowers into
the web of grass,

watching it push back. In my grandfather's legs
sure as aspens

among squat stones.
Shapes of the Cross. There,

look: Sophie and
Joseph Bucharski.

In lichen rust.
The cracked slab.

Бу-чар-скі

       In the land heaving around us
like an ocean.

The faintest rim of the city. The fresh crop foisted
on the bare back of Clover Bar,

moating refinery to highway, false brick
to vinyl armour. Under the flare stacks,

stitching the off-ramps, the whiff of open,
of birchroot, the shrieks

of long-necked birds field to shore.
      The welting chant of roadsigns:

Crane Drive, Birch Street,
      Cree Road.

Swear that when we get to the farm
you won't look at the engine blocks leeching the yard,

the junk-heaped back forty,
                              the rotting lumber,

the piles of cow dung,
the cattle loose,

        and never mind the derelict siding,
        ripped drapes over the windows,

                the screen door dangling. Swear
        you won't look too long. No telling

whether some gimped-up patriarch will come out
with a rifle.

Look what they've done.
Look at the garden.

> *It used to be so nice,*
> > *the rose bushes. The sweet peas.*

> *Now look. Oil wells in the crocuses.*
> *All the rye would suck from Pa's body*

> > *there. Books would appear. A thousand*

> *bucks per oilwell per month times six oilwells.*
> How could anyone here turn that down?

To be born knowing the bells of St. George ringing for the dead,
the smoke thrown in living faces each Sunday,

      the sickening incense swinging.
    Then to get doused with water

holy because it's not from around here,
                      and eating and drinking

just symbols of a more important life lost,
and you must stand,

stand, keep aimed in the right direction,
for patience shall reap all manner of

                          gifts when the time comes.

Knowing that once the crops gather all they're owed —
wheat heads to the wind, tomatoes

      hardening under a blue sun,
          asking softly for the books to balance —

a grand per month per oilwell times six oilwells.
Wringing out the thought that soon

      the clouds will pay up. Mouthing out the thought
that soon as it all goes right we'll all be laughing.

Yet so sure of this

radio dragging range roads, abandoned campgrounds,
fresh cop tracks and coyote tracks, through the wailing

tunnel of night.
So sure of the shitmix in water bottles between the knees in the backseat,

unleashed in clatter-toothed
huddles on some shopkid's back forty,

the floodlight over the barn stuck strafing each fortified cluster.
So sure of the give of tailgates,

of ditches, the willingness of engines, the stiffness
of parkas

braced against the wish for day and vinyl siding,
against the far gibberish of fuel

along the gridways,
against the family dog, against the wild dog.

So sure that it all means
nothing, *Бучарскі*.

Counting on the Ranger, the Rover, the F-250
lined along the tin-snake shed of the curling club.

It's here you'll be able to concentrate
on take-outs, see to the pulse of your lines,

      whittle the right kind of wrist tension
for a chance in the tourney — maybe hit the circuit,

              win a couple bucks,
              build a sandbox for the boys,

            throw some asphalt on the driveway,
             hell,

might even win a plane ride south for a week
        in winter, get acquainted with that big,

slow-curving line from A to B
           that everyone keeps talking about.

I swear, hardship these days is the endurance
of atrophy. See those women

on break outside Derwent High School —
now a window blind factory, cultivating jobs in the bookless

classrooms of industry —
gymnasium lifebreath enterprise, entrepreneurial

smoke-breaks, or not —

those women in front of the school,
they have the same devout braids,

the same homemade blouses under company windbreakers,
the same empty hands.

Note how they don't speak to us. Maybe they're made
to wear uniforms. Blind into blind-slot,

factory vinyl,
promise of supper and a walk to work, not bad,

blind into blind-slot all week
in a town of two hundred,

blinds tumbling out the cutter.
What should we make

of these women, their flashing,
vacant hands. Their paycheques.

The tavern sown tight into all our chests
as we stand beyond its galvanized embrace

beside the rail line — this track of weeds and mud —
rearing up hard won and mint green

at the open end of Main Street, a square-box spooked horse,
woeful and regular. Trailblazer, Silverado, F-150

tuned to the tavern sign. *Come home*,
she says. Will always say.

Imagine waking halfway home.
　　The sun jet-straight, the grass jagged.

Scar tissue a child's drawing
　　of the line splitting road from ditch —

the split cheek, missing digits,
your wheels along this road,

　　　　　　　just accidents.
This road with its nervous skiffs of gravel.

　　　Quackgrass, blanket flowers
　　stitching roots through its ditches,

barn swallows tethered to strings of startled grasshoppers.
You could swear

your tires were aimed at the fog of city lights on the horizon.
You didn't have a prayer.

　　　　　　All that wind migrating the topsoil in tangled threads,
coyote jogging head down along the shoulder,

　　　　　　　steam huffing from his nostrils and the barbed wire
strung loose to keep the cattle out

or in, spread carcasses of trees from tornado seasons,
　　　　　　　　all those rocks pilgriming back to the field,

the same damn thing every year.

Along this backroad

    to where the grain elevator was,
over land sliced into thinkable grids and made to work.

See the split souls not knowing the earth's tongue
but plunging

seeds into it anyway.
The water oozing a map too deep to read.

If you could swear on the ghost-thuds of buffalo,
       paskwâwimostos.

             If you could swear on the worms and societies of ants
through these hard-packed onion layers,

      swear on the high combines
running numbers over the stubbled surface,

and on the road
      as abacus, assuming something

brief — your only choice this road —
       assuming something resembling prosperity.

Now see this hamlet's welcome sign,
stained and restained

and the playground housing its
lethal equipment,

one strip mall and one regular mall and the Franklin's Inn.
Then subdivision,

the gobbling of exhausted farmland.
Some developer

leaning thinly on symbols,
on heroics,

richest suburb in the province because the refineries
fell within our jurisdiction,

hell,
that's why the first houses were built,

the industry growing out the ass-end of Edmonton,
the handiness of oil and pulp and steel,

not needing to pray on seeds or weather or cattle,
how most people's parents had prayed.

These cedar shakes,
the pastel siding, stacked wide. See this hamlet,

the largest in the world
for tax purposes,

site of blissful childhoods,
slapped into a suburb proper,

and our hero still stands in a tree over the seventh hole, still flies
over an eastern wood calling forth the developers.

See this Robin Hood give and give.
To this house, a fig tree arching at the bay window

      from within its net of lights.
In front of this house, a tricycle,

          a satellite dish.
Out of this house, the old lady now

      walking her beer cans to the trash bin in the park.
In this house, a football ref

with coke-bottle glasses and legions of rose bushes.
In this one, an English professor will give up

and amass arrowheads and jazz records.
Into this house we can't imagine

for the foil over the windows.
      This house, two stories tall, impossible to see.

In this one, Stevie Ray Vaughan
        and the woman always a mess.

      In this one, the neighbours come over
and stay till morning.

At this one, the kids won't come
inside until the dad's home from work.

         This house refuses to shear the yard these days.
         This house dries bedsheets on the verandah at night.

In this one, a man beats his dog with a broom handle.
Out front of this one, an old guy waters his driveway.

In back of this one, there's always a rink when it's cold.
This house keeps their garbage bins out front

and a stake and a chain for a missing dog.
Out of this house there's pipesmoke and a woodstove,

        a big beard, a library.
In front of this one, gnomes and flamingos.

In this one, a girl shaved her head.
In this house, no Christmas,

        no birthdays, the weirdest boy.
In this house, a fat kid plots his revenge,

     shimmering and Romanian.
        See this house neighbouring the basement preschool,

letting the kids scream in their yard after.
Tell everyone this house always smells

         of old potatoes.
Tell this one always with milk on the doorstep.

      Say this house, its one-eyed tabby
arching at the window. Say the fig tree within its net of lights.

Their house was a joust between onion and garlic.
Their house of lukewarm bathwater, of Friday night laundry,

invisible guilt, soup on the stove.
A Texas mickey of rye,

dirt under the fingernails,
the spring thaw she crawled through when the steel rod

pierced her abdomen on the farm alone —
I just have to make it to the road. Their house

of yarn and roses, crab apples, zucchini,
old grass clippings in a garbage bag. Silent struggling,

sitting with this love, this greying habit,
and buried amid all these mistakes.

This stripmall carwash, the sand and butts, the lot dozed almost clean.
These plumes of exhaust, these asses frozen curb-sitting the Mac's,

clean rows of Caravans huffing wax-soap,
these jumpy exits from the carwash. See? They can't see us. These lips

around a cache of cast-offs caked in road grit and rocky-road lipstick.
See a girl jump up to polish a hood, to mug a yes-maam-no-maam,

headlights flaring her into a road risk and you can't trust that woman's foot on
    her brake
the unlit eyes. See this girl saying *I'll take you to the cleaners. Just try it.*

See the impoverishment of mazework between our childhood houses,
the farming narratives breaking open all around us,

the incantatory stoplight timers of the heart lurched out of whack.
Miming how we've been taught to use the head and hands

to calibrate our propriety over yard, swingset and shrubbery, or how much
right we have to stand at the side of the highway with a bedsheet

that says *Honk if You Miss the Trees* in one hundred magic markers,
and how the trees are stacked up in a crazed and useless pile ready for the
    chipper

behind the fringe they left around the perimeter of the lot to keep us sated,
and the Pontiac dealership that sits there now, streetlit so bright

the whole hamlet can't see the stars it used to. Remember: the torso's
where the sweet and vital meat is lodged.

Remember the fists of industry, the shanghaied carburetor
of identity distilling a tune

we can hum at the light, a way to train our gaze to lengthen into the distance,
to make us look right and wise to each other

along the three lanes leading to the city, past the fluorescent Pontiac dealership —
Batoche, Canada, Britain, Hairy Hill, Semans, York,

Derwent, Strathcona, Mallaig: what could these mean?
Remember, we're parked here by debt and need and after that,

who knows. Maybe the way the sky presses concave like a sheet of glass,
the fact we got stories here, the degree to which we want

or warrant the names we hold in mind in the warmth of the too-long stoplight.
Maybe the way we drift back home to rest at the end of every day.

And his planting early. Waiting till the frost
lifts and the sun's first tilt over the backyard.

Means the beets'll be good for pulling mid-August.
Means the house in the city throwing shadows of farm:

deep dust in the drapes, the canning on homemade shelves,
the beets that pulled us to the garden's edge.

Hearing *I never got nothing from farming.*
The rough knives to boards scored with onion,

the oil of his wife's hands, the bloody pink root, accordion stains —
Kolomayka, Bukovina, how do they go, Pa?

Means his harmonica's a sparrow. Appearing
and receding. Seeing his sleeves rolled to the elbow,

the twitch in his hands,
how he lifts and presses the melody.

На щаця на здоровя на новей рік!
I threw wheat in her doorway and spoke in her lilt.

She was born on the coldest day of the year,
New Year's Eve on the old calendar.

The letters, they came like uncracked code.
Foreign cousins starving in Lviv, photos of a baby.

She rolls dollar bills into the fingers of gloves
and her pencil sketching characters, traced till perfect.

She draws her children, sisters and grandchildren. Never herself.
At her elbow a Scot-named child with a longing for boxy Cyrillic.

The children in the readers have sleds and ponies.
They're gulping water from the stream with a cupped hand.

Her hand steady around the stylus in spring,
tough beeswax, field symbols on the *писанки*,

eternity in wax lines, wheat sheaves for bounty,
curls of protection, green dye for hope and the new crop.

And the professor teaches new Ukrainian, Kiev Ukrainian,
clean S sounds, weightless V's. I speak S's the width of toothpicks.

And she waves her arm of wet soil and crochet hooks and raspberry canes.
And she says, *What's the point. It's a dying language.*

And it's not the onion, it's the knife, three for a buck at the dollar store,
serrated in China, one side only.

And the recipe cut from a thriftstore magazine,
Cabbage Potato Soup.

And it's the knife that's doing it, my hand
that's breaking the cage of white,

ringed flesh, loosing juice that makes the eyes make water.
And it's my grandmother's kitchen,

its earthen *цибуля* reek,
her hand on the wooden spoon,

spoon turning the borshch,
resurrecting,
resurrecting,
the beets at the bottom

becoming the beets at the top.
It's her flowered blouse, her elbows

propped on the other side of the counter.
And telling me I'm doing it all wrong.

And offering to help but she can't figure out how
to work the knife.

But it's okay, she says,
because look at the beautiful picture

on the recipe.
Just look at what you're making.

Night ticking into place.
Swells of empty field before me,

the bleachers' ribs, the chainlink's diamond cuts,
the ball no one plays.

Two skateboarders doodling margins on a backdrop wild with garry oak.
I strain,

returning the moon's blank gaze,
mind curled, deking pattern,

the chainlink's diamond cuts, the small kid's small-wheeled
song,

which is the moon, I see now,
once he cracks an axle jumping a simple sewer grate,

once he throws his board,
                        blue and spinning,

back to the trees.
How place invades the body. The sod,

the pavement lodged inside the ribcage.
Throat doused with bitter canola,

sad flax, a song
I don't know how to sing.

Singing anchor or paperweight,
story or bone.

Asking my mother,
a barefoot child running the swathed field,

fully Ukrainian,
frowning with maturity in all the photos.

Asking the first books
appearing to her in school, in English.

Asking them like escape.
Knowing now she's portioning canola fields,

making people fill out all the permits
before they build.

Variegated bungalows. Fifty years.
Something about need and order.

Something about how that man
tries to push the bulging links of the fence back

into place
                        while he waits for a bus,

his working concert of leg muscles.
Something about how that pigeon hawk

holds its body over the crow,
          a squeeze

of talons until the head
quits twitching,

                              and the squeezing after death.
And how they do this at the shore

of an ocean of traffic.
Waves loud as bedlam.

If there's calm in belonging.
Like when there's a storm and the power goes out:

if there's a thinning, nothing to do but look out your window,
the trees that make you,

bending. Cacophony of throat and ribcage; the lodged
song out of tune.

Something about need and order. And loss can behave like blessing,
but it's always loss.

Remembering cedar and mountain ash. Remembering maple and poplar,
lilac, juniper, conifer, larch,

spruce trees green and blue. The aspen sentinels.
Birch, *береза*, *li boloo*, *le bouleau*, *waskway*. Then a sumac.

Remembering geese moving, lake to park,
swaying the air between eavestroughs,

down mazestreets, over poplars and cedars,
over the gullets of wrens and magpies.

Standing there, under the bodies of geese —
the long swish of air through wing,

air pushed through rope throats, calls caught
and kept — foreign acorns landing with small

wooden cracks on driveways and rolling
to the dry hug of earth.

                              Kneeling in the vertigo of lawn.
The thickened sun. The crows

that lance through trash bins fat with bags of dog shit
in a soup of light and the pushed-away that blots

desire as it digs for nematodes in the clay
                           beneath,

the slidewhistle screams of seagull, the flurry of moved air,
crowstab, oakdrop, skygrey

bellies honking through the mind and the reasons one
digs to get to them.

Chasing a jackrabbit home in the car at night, down Nottingham Road
and into the crescent — your sixth left — looking for the motorized

deer on the lawn
of the corner house in the winter; in spring

you're on your own
to memorize the shapes of trees.

Never startling one from its nest
while we sat in the shrubs

and wood chips of the park and chugged from two-litres
of raspberry cooler, never when my brother and I

were hooked on badminton or boomerang or straight catch
for three weeks in the summer, never

when I trudged to and from the bus, the half-hour trip to the university
taking three hours and all angles and manners of light.

Always on the road I found them. The shock
of fleeing underfur, its left eye on me when it finally stops

to let me pass: you wouldn't think it could kick
the life from your chest if you had a mind to get close enough.

And a magpie clamping down on the edge of the furthest twig
and jumping,

jumping, breaking it free and flying off. Diving at that fat
kid Frank's head

until he dropped his ice cream in the middle of Evergreen
Street and ran for the garage.

Amassing such a beakful of trash from the mall dumpster,
such a haul of lettuce from the Safeway.

Crowing at a dead one in the ditch,
the jut of its head,

downward, over and over.
Distracted from drinking

by her image in a puddle.
Hopping the length of the quad.

With no tail feathers. With a worm,
with a nut. Ganging up on a hawk

as it nears their nest.
Trying to pull the ring off its ankle.

Returning as a hummingbird to show her she's still watching.
Some treason of embodiment, some betrayal of feather.

Some hollow bone.
Some quivering miracle on a dewy morning,

early summer,
as my mother's out in the yard clipping sweet peas,

the feeling that the world has clicked to rightness for once,
bridged to otherness,

swollen violins at the end of the movie,
my mom would be okay:

her mother was okay and around to see.
The way the hummingbird lingered tightly in front of her

as she walked back to the house with her hands full
of every colour of sweet pea imaginable.

And she was there.
They were walking together.

Whistling. Maybe

when the wild rose hooks to the skin.

Maybe rearing back, a gasp, a slapping of thighs,
summoning the dance of allotment,

the tap-tapping of the heartbeat against the wind-drenched air.

Full of gangrene, here in the trees.

Wide and parasitic,
gutting the thick, buried veins of the mushrooms,

and the trail of hawk shadowing the path,

and the deer behind the clearing,
wishing for weightlessness.

Crowing *What's the use of your breath then.*
Why did you come here.

Maybe placing the ear against the radiator.

Holding through the heat and it broadcasting.

Hammer taps against a kneebone. Pings of light through swinging prisms.
A calm within the crumbling walls of the body.

Trying to match those strains with an accordion,

pale green as grass escaping mud. In the night a C chord, held,
walling itself in,

and the music behind what's there, is squirming,
knowing nothing.

Knowing that C chord is you. Holding patterns of grief
plodding the morning's empty parking lot to face the day's traffic.

Knowing

you'll kneel and press your ear to a patch of ground. Listening
for the earth's heartbeat beyond the world's muffling door,

its accordion breath, its hammer-taps, its

desired, untraffickable light

hurtling through from the east, the pond
buzzing with large birds, small birds,

no bread crumbs in your pockets.

Home calling like a horn through fog.
Your hands lifting and circling the plain of your lap.

A candle doused with slough water.

Laughter like pots crashing:
you never thought it could be so beautiful.

Behind you, sun; in front, water.
Remembering the east side of the old yard,

how one grandmother's life
flamed into the doctrine of cattle

and children. That lilac
bush by the garden is how the tears fell.

And along the west fence by the shed another grandmother
gazed over the tramped Saskatchewan fairground

at the man she would marry.
The chainlinks along the back,

let's say that's Canada. See the row of sweet peas climbing.
Say this birch was planted so

the memory of grandmothers can climb and gain vantage.

The earthworms I took to the garage after school —
their pieces writhed so differently away.

Say my father is sitting on the roof.
Every childhood dog, every car he ever had, looking.

And say I'm three, crouched in the yard like someone
trying to peel reason from above.

Say the big spruce came down before
or after the picture, or say it's still there,

upwardly-assertive, sap-starved and churning up the sewer pipes,
shading my brother's bedroom window.

Now say *It was a different big tree that left.*
Maybe the poplar by the garage.

Maybe in some groove of needle or spawn of cone
my brother is still five and home

from kindergarten with the flu, sweet-speaking,
cherub-rough, puffy eyes and a cowlick,

for once not smarter than me. Maybe
just five and tucked in to read *Harry the Dirty Dog.*

Maybe our house on Fir Street,
someone's fifth of an acre, someone's protective thicket

is where I'm three and crouching,
looking up at Dad while he smiles out at his wife and the camera

and the grass is softer than grass between my toes.

Could we find that place, that slough at the curve of what road
that we'd visit in the van in the summer,

with its weeping branches like the walls of a top-lit room,
the sky like a skylight, the red-winged blackbirds

as present as peacocks and the insects deafening?

Where Dad would quiet the engine so we could watch
and we could listen and let the scene press into our memory.

Not the name or place. There'd be nothing
for the computer when we are older

and want to find it.

A storm's coming in,
the wind a kilometre away and gaining.

I'm on the blank bleachers;
I can hear it,

a tidal conch unfolded, blasting the trees — four hundred metres away —

here it comes, it's dark
and the first spits of rain slap the street at the far end

of the park, the gust bowls into the clearing — ten metres —
rattles

the fence that pens in the diamond, joggles
loose

the fenceposts, scoops out my ears and borrows my breath and
I am electrocuted stubbornpinned I can't

hope to rise to the sky or swim the charged
air I know

less about this place
and its winds, this city on this island, than I know about baseball

and I don't give a fuck

about baseball.
That was just the first gust.

Radio storm callers shouting for more through the night,
more noise to the east and what does it mean

when the wind comes from the east here —
here comes the second gust —

I heard somewhere it means storms, the worst ones, the ground wobblers,
and this was the figurehead,

the bowsprit, the cutwater — I had to look those words up —
I'll be gone before I can learn —

goddamn kid moves twice a year
Dad says — leaving storms and parts of boats and off goes the gale

rounding the big hill, Mount Doug, Hill of Cedars,
rain that rends

the ground to mush, rain
that sounds like static through a long, long record needle,

rain that pricks whorls
onto head and into hands.

There goes the third —

see the infield flying off after it
in spirals

violently, teaspoon by
teaspoon by teaspoon.

Remember need and order,
how in May the brown stubble rolls off in every direction.

 Oy bojy, used to be if you needed to pay
 so much

 as a speeding ticket you had to take yourself all the way
 into town, eighty-second and a hundred

 and fifth, to the old post office
 building there, and praise

the skies you don't have to
bother with that anymore because who

has time for a half-day in some lineup?
People weren't so busy back then,

mind you, and if you told your boss you had
to go pay a goddamn speeding ticket he'd let you

go 'cause there he'd be, standing in that same
lineup the next week.

It's changed now, that street.
Frivolous things. Cafés and bars, *bojy*,

so many bars, the train station turned into a bar,
and bookstores — who has time to read books?

I wish I had that kind of time.
That Southpark dealership is still there.

That carwash, Bubbles. Army & Navy.
It's all changed. And someday that lot

where the Esso used to be
it will be clean and ready for a building

and just you wait what it's going to be.
Another bar. Some kind fancy patio.

Used to be that street had a use.
Because you know why we've got the jaywalking law

and the slam-on-your-brakes-
for-pedestrians law and the price of a speeding ticket is so goddamn high?

It was that concert at the baseball field north of the river,
2001. Not even that. It was how the cops forced everyone leaving

that concert across the High Level bridge and onto Whyte
just as they were calling last call.

That's how you make riots
on Canada Day. Now you can't walk three feet

without running into a cop on a Saturday evening in the summertime.
They were just waiting for an excuse.

Bojy, these suburbanites,
these football stars and girls dressed like escorts,

the future businesspeople of the world bloating the nighttime economy,
renting stretch SUVs to go line the gutters with their vomit,

dropping their garbage on the sidewalks,
their pristinely empty heads,

their money in loose balls thrown at one place and the next,
pissed off and cackling and fighting and screaming and crying.

In the daytime, their mothers shopping in the boutiques,
dodging their own children's vomit, trading

on stories of destiny, of angels. You can count on one hand
the number of real things or real people.

Hub Cigar is dying.
That guy who lives in the Commie,

Doug or Don, you see him around some.
That Native guy used to sell copies of *Our Voice* at the corner,

in front of, what is it, that Chicken Scratch place,
across from the fucking Chapters.

And we were in the basement of the Empress
Hotel, staring at hundred-year-old soaps

and dance programs from dominion holidays.
And it was New Year's Eve, 1925: crab cocktail, breast of pheasant,

glazed pineapple and champagne.
And my mother was tsking the polished floor and the set table.

And all the women were dressed like nurses lined in a grim row.
It could've been her, could've been me, on our hands and knees.

And Dad just kept strolling the long hallway whistling, indelible gas jockey stroll,
not betraying shock, admiration, disdain,

or anything at all.
Here lies a fishing hole.

And here lie scattered firs and woodsmoke,
all these royal menus under glass.

And I was thinking about Ontario, about the night they took the ashtrays away,
some bartender I'd never seen stacking them up,

crook of the elbow,
saying hereafter we must poison ourselves elsewhere,

bullshit little smirk saying *the state's a bitch ain't it,*
one second you're legal and the next, well, hey.

And you loving it there.
Like catching a guy skating up the middle with his head down,

like steel guitar
or folks your grandmother's age.

Like those lonesome songs that keep scooping out your insides, or someone
wailing through the open window

about twenty-five below,
or wine stains on the snow

and on the carpet. I was thinking about that night two regulars,
hair yellowed, tipped their glasses

together and nodded like they'd never see each other again.
And I'll bet they never did.

Night stretching over my field, moth-bitten and complete.
I'm wary now of its too-perfect geometry, its bevel over the wide earth.

Vantaged in this containered city block,
how does triangulation work

on this field I've got going, when just to be splitting a case of beer
is creative, just to be sharing a room, speaking at length,

how can all these stars track across the sky like that?
Geese split some exotic hard-shelled grain in imagined daylight —

no chronology in this mindfield, so it folds quickly back to night —
and they nestle as fur-bearers nestle in the stubbled, uncertain plain.

Each goose hugging itself with its own loose neck
and sleeping.

Let's say

I can't feel stars like this in my bones
anymore — without really stretching,

sending the phalangeal
bits as far

away from the head as possible,

holding tight and loose at once —
the kind of stars too thickly flocked for contours

or selfness,

that are there in the fielded sky of the head.
Let's say I'm asking how to get

to a field from here.

Looking up at the orange night.
One dot, two dot.

And an ache like the poverty of old juice on a store-shelf,
for a moment. Then it's not.

Then it's just how it goes. One dot, two dot.
Those sweet few that made it here.

And all the fields recalled with a roving,
improvised clarity.

I'll go back in and sit on the bed and not speak.
I'll leave a bulb on in the hope the moth can find it.

And entering Lanigan, second night on the bus. Lightning
forking at the staggering flat.

And it's them, I'm sure, telling me it's time.
The driver's big arms pulling us into falling always falling towns.

There's the Ez-Wall Motel's busted door frames,
the closed-up train station, the old grocery store

where all the cashiers knew Grandpa's name,
the café where Grandma baked muffins,

buckets, buckets of saskatoons and a hunchback mutt
staring from the gravel lot of the ice cream shop biggest scoops

I've ever seen I swear that mutt
stares us right out of town

to where I know the rest by heart and pass

through each just as fast: Guernsey, Plunkett,
the potash mine,

Viscount, Colonsay, Elstow, Clavet.
Yes. I'm watching.

Oh the grief of mothers,
your shortness on the phone all summer.

Strafe of questions in place of self,
oh your head always down at your desk at work

and your daughter lives so far, so far,

you don't know what her house looks like,
what sort of bed she lies in at night,

where she laughs or does her thinking.

Oh how you secret your grief until it flees too large and fresh,
oh you didn't know the sun would be so white at this turn of your life.

Now you pick up and cradle the newspaper

and wonder where you've gone.
Where, oh where have these red eyes come from.

Oh grief, said your mother at the stove

when you told her you'd marry that Protestant,
some long-hair telling round, brown-eyed stories about his dog and Saskatchewan.

The eyes of your children, oh grief, she said,
he's missing some teeth and you barely know him.

She thought you were gone to her.
Ripping the female line. All the ways one must leave.

And loss, your mother, your maybe daggerous daughter,

oh how alone you are here,
how helpless in this repetition

on the gurney
with your family all around.

Band of snow under horizon's lip, the boots on the fenceposts
west of town or your parents'

shyness at cameras. These are yours.
You're not floating and you haven't been asleep.

    Eight years old and you're bringing in the cows —
    the blond hair, the frown, bear no resemblance

    to the face
that follows you to the hospital.

You know the years of your surgeries for the form:
the C sections, the knee.

You go straight for your health card, fingers quick through the wallet.
If you take too long that might go in your file.

Your signature shortened, quaking.
Questions like shots of vodka, *na zdorovya* —

   where do you live, who do you work with, the tie the doctor wears, Mom,
   the pen he writes with. What did we do today —

clockhands grip the bowl of the spinning world,
keep the machines ticking regular. The hollow of your face

each time you look at them
anew.

Hard mauve flowers in the dead brown grass.
The lake housed sky-like at the bottom of the field.

Glacial blue, solid, floating meadow lake.
A quiet that redraws the sack of self.

You are alone here. You gaze across swells of chaff
at stands of twiggy poplars, the cemetery, the unmoving blue,

and down again at one crocus's yolky centre.
    Under the bowtie of the neurologist, it makes sense

    you'd find yourself here, looking down at the bright gown
    and up again, it makes sense every time you find yourself.

Into our eyes the blank of fresh panic:
will the gauzed buds spread underneath?

    Nothing, except this pain at the top of the head —
peach-sized, present-tensed. *Nothing but that,* you say.

A fallow field.
The wild depression of earth,

the grief of mothers.
You've stopped believing

there are stars that poke through the universe —
    this pain, this new pressure at the top of your head —

    who can you tell here, parked in the corner of this ward,
    the green uniforms and units of husband, daughter and son

    among the hard-fought chairs tossed off like peelings,
    the tests, the bags of fluid

    beeping noise and fluorescent light.

Dear universe, dear rocks, bugs, birds, field, earth:
listen:

>four cops peer through a window in a door
>into a room that holds a violent man.

>You'll ask why they're there,
>standing outside the door from fear

>or ready to turn and stare at you next.
>Listen: the man in that room has nothing

>to do with this.

There's a span of sun. The eyes of the crocuses
follow it.

You're sitting in the field whether my grandmother fixes the tractor
somewhere behind you or not.

Spring teeters on its lip and the lake is far from solid —
stare hard: the lake, the flower. See their ions buzzing still.

What happened was you sobbed your pathways closed.
Blood didn't flood the brain right and here we are.

Stress, the echo chamber of the ex-Catholic.

We took turns sobbing over how we've separated our lives,
how I've ripped the female line, and it didn't happen to me

like it happened to you.
Every fear took every chair around the table,

clutched our berry-stained fingers,
and their faces were too perfect.

I was here for once to yell at you,
poor-platformed, needfully. It was the sun,

it was the poison of too much or not enough.

You became an asteroid. You plunged into the cold pool
of hours and months,

and your metals were nothing
the world could've imagined.

A million miles, your little vacuum path.
You entered like a bubble being shaped,

and it's easier than two kids lunging for a ball in dead fallow —
overlooking the graveyard of people with your names — to forget.

Then you're thirteen, and there's a chance the ficus muscling in the corner
of the parental front room, stealing all the best particulates from the dusted air,

could know more — yet this body, yet this hate and North American love,
this is real. You want to want what little there is to know at thirteen.

At thirteen, you measure the same height as this woman lost and clawing back.
Too young, too big to know what shoes are right for the occasion.

The eyes of the fathers in town as you wait for yours outside the bar.
The eyes of people's sons, the mouths of daughters.

At thirteen, you keep your hair in place but aren't one to sleep over the edge
of chesterfields, to sleep standing up, to sleep awake.

You hate. You think.
You wear plaid skirts but no nylons, broaches on your sweaters.

You could break into a sprint at any time.
Your eyes acquiesce, disapprove of the whole planted world.

Hands tensed and fingers unpainted — you'd practice three-pointers
if someone threw you a ball. In the front room,

before the narrative eye of the camera.
Your mother's lips red like a brake light.

Your own lips almost smiling, but for the eyes,
standing shoulder to shoulder with your father, matching his look.

I've learned that to jump the hospital breadline, start crying,
go with the body,

report memory loss, the grief of mothers and daughters and the world
will spin out with grabbing arms.

Time in a line, a combine, a crop duster.

We're all here; terrified for you. We sleep in parked cars,
eat the food of any offering machine.

We send feelers into all the upper corners of all the rooms,
across phone lines, we collect receipts

and proper names and search for numbness
as they test you. The hippocampus records, which means nothing.

I'll take your picture with the newspaper
to show you, over and over.

A cruel thing, these repetitions.
You'd never believe it.

So glib, the date printed in the top right corner,
like anyone could just know. The line of the IV,

low ticking in near darkness,
the farthest window. If you can conjure crocuses,

the contingency of flowers, then it's just a needle in the same groove,
then we can empty our pockets.

The gridmaps of cities, the parcels of fields from the sky.
They clench you, making your nose bleed in the dry night.

Your love moulds the edges of every grief, seeks and forgets
all wisdom, commensurate with the dread of your childhood.

Your father takes one hand, gathers up the hard grass in the cemetery,
stirs the hard light, aims at the identical death dates on the stones.

The distance between *wisit* and visit. *Orkadock* and orthodox.
Dizzy from the journeys we've made. We try to let the distance pass.

An ocean of lecture hall desks, relief of city. Story of your mother's burning school.
Do you remember your mother is not here as you lie under monitors.

Spanish flu, he says. You remember the term blue baby,
the furrowed soil of the brows of grown relations.

Even from a great distance, what doesn't leave is intonation,
which syllables you lean on. The way you say "I don't be*lieve* it."

A car can't be silent past the farmyards; its edges aren't hard
like white light or range roads. An engine meets the wilding gaze of cattle.

You finally sleep. The dark soil of your brow. Certain you just woke up.
These things don't leave. They fill the room like mist or blood.

Repetition of flight. Flee, return. A book, a car, a hospital bed.
We're all here, groggy, fitful, urging you again to let the distance pass.

Dad looks down and rubs his eyes, looks up again.
Says, *No, you haven't slept, and it's time.*

He's not equipped to laugh anymore. You've bought up all his good
Saskatchewan patience but there's always more

and this makes you feel normal.
Just close your eyes, no growth in your questions, *Rest,*

he says.
The way you talk to each other like I'm not in the room makes me so relieved.

I'd ask but the lights are out in this new room with no beds but a door,
and it's my turn to stagger for the car.

I'd ask,
Did you grow canola? Did you grow wheat? Alfalfa? Oats?

How many cattle did you bring from the fields after school, Mom?
Where did you graze them?

How light were your steps around your father
like a toddler on the kitchen floor?

I'd ask everything twice, two thousand times.
I'd never get tired of the answer.

Maybe a bubble burst your mind or a curtain fell,
maybe a vein will slack the muscles of your face.

You're so quiet. Maybe I live here now.
Crossing back into this place and landing hard.

Maybe you forget I'm just visiting.
Maybe I'll never see you again.

Maybe this is new and forever.
You ask again from within your bowl of earth: *what happened.*

I say I don't know.
One minute you were here.

I'll sit with you.
We'll watch the rough hawk through the constant morning —

its feathers split from the bone, from the west wind.
We can sit and keep making it so.

    Somewhere you're crossing the quad with your hair done.
    Your shoes are polished.

Look how the crow appears, its ghost and chase.
The turnoff tracing up to your parents' farm,

thickened by unshorn poplar
or birch or fir.

    Somewhere I tell you again that those cops are there
    for the violent man and not for you.

Furred copper on the roof of the old leaning shed.
No straight lines

but the ones cut by the road crews and the threshing crews
and even then —

    Somewhere the sobs fly from me, disembodied;
    you're all on the other side of airport security.

No one knows me where we sit;
I'm not like the birch;

spores bloom from the dirt like new continents;
I'm my own brightened gaze across the grasses of property.

Somewhere you shake my future father's hand
and the snowplows deafen and his car is five seconds from stalling.

Your forehead holds no crease here but one down the middle,
yet you smile and watch the hawk and I can see how you'll age in this white light.

Somewhere I'm telling you to go to hell
as you leave to do some shitty secretary job.

What will we do here — I come with that.
Let's climb to vantage, let's cross the lip,

let's put our arms out and undulate with the ground's waving.
Somewhere you tell me to turn up the stereo and the floor's already shaking.

It wouldn't be like you not to try — to advocate for trying.
Trying to push saplings from a felled tree.

Somewhere your mother crochets a tablecloth,
her nose packed with Vicks and Dallas on her small TV set.

A felled tree can stitch itself upright here.
Tell me what kind of bird that is.

A smirk and near-silence as you put your mouth around the word.
Somewhere a hawk lifts a mouse

from the wealth of grass and
you laugh and turn to me —

The sun resurfacing as we know it does
as I rise from the backseat of the car.

Chickadees and seagulls shaking out the parking lot.
I'm running for the building.

You've excavated these hours.
    Your face is different,

which is to say, the same, getting closer,
a glass filling, the wind picking up;

you're walking across the field and down the hill toward the highway,
you're sitting up in bed, asking the source of the holy bruises

on the insides of your elbows,
asking what happened through the night.

Was there a night. How much time and distance.
How did you guess the right direction.

What was the right direction.
How did you know to hold your gown closed

as I walked you to the bathroom.
Did you fall down, hit your head.

Was it like a drunken blackout;
your father waking up on the floor with an equivalent loss.

You feel shame. Your son shakes his head:
you were present; you were absent.

Dad mumbles *broken record*, and his laugh
is like all the laughs I've heard.

We take the roads slow and get lost
leaving the hospital.

Silence swarming with intention.
Getting back on the tow-rope of time.

   I wonder if you remember the day before;
   how I yelled.

The radio is terrible. Every overburdened melody,
every heartless word.

Will this be forgotten.
I'll go back east.

We'll keep to the normalcy
of grief. Like

scenery passing.
Yesterday's newspaper

in the back seat.
Old cups of coffee in their holders.

Your son's getting married next week
and you know this,

you do. The sky has always been wide.
The ground still undulates once you get off the highway.

Look out your window,
Mom. Look how the land rolls along beside us.

Notes

page 6: *néhiyawak*, "the Cree people."

page 7: *Bolishi, Moatiski, Drogowich*, three cities in Poland, presumably. The poet has since learned that Drogowich is Drohobych, a city in the west of modern Ukraine, and birthplace of writer and artist Bruno Schulz, whose unjust death occurred there too.

page 12: catcha mayesh / Як ся маєш: the Cyrillic is pronounced "Yak she mayesh." It means "How are you?"

page 17: *pohanyn*, "pagan"; similar words include the adjective *pohanyj*, meaning "bad," and the verb *pohanyty*, meaning "to soil." Lines have been taken from Andrew Suknaski's poems "Winnipeg to Saskatoon/Night Journey" and "Leaving Home Again" from *In the name of Narid* (The Porcupine's Quill, 1981). Suknaski would often refer to himself in the third-person, as "suknatskyj," in his poems.

page 19: Бу-чар-скі, pronounced "Bucharski."

page 30: *paskwâwimostos*, Cree for "buffalo."

page 38: *На щаця на здоровя на новей рік*! Pronounced "Na shcha-shchya na zdorovya na novay reek," and meaning, "To happiness and health in the new year." (See "*na zdorovya*" on p. 69, a Ukrainian toast.)

     писанки, the Cyrillic writing of "pysanky," or Ukrainian Easter eggs.

page 39: *цибуля*, pronounced "tsyboolya," meaning "onion."

page 44: Birch, *береза*, *li boloo*, *le bouleau*, *waskway*. All these words mean "birch," in English, Ukrainian, Michif, French, and Cree.

page 55: *Oy bojy*, Ukrainian for "Oh God."

Acknowledgements

Thank you to mentors and teachers Dionne Brand, Tim Lilburn, Lorna Crozier, Rhea Tregebov, and Elise Partridge for teaching me how to see and hear. Thank you to editor Harold Rhenisch and publisher Paul Wilson for seeing and hearing something in these poems. Thank you to heroes Andrew Suknaski, Fred Wah, Dennis Lee, and Jan Zwicky, whose books became totems while I was making these poems. Endless thanks to Dianne, Bill, Jason, Rayna, Mason, Sarah, Erin, Garry, Jeanne, Peter, Heather, Terry, to the memories of Mary, Catherine, and Norman, and to all the Grahams, Bucharskis, Bykewiches, and Hillises. And thank you to Mark Jull, who knows I can do no other.

This book benefited from the monetary assistance of the Social Sciences and Humanities Research Council and the Ontario Arts Council.

Versions of the poems in this collection have appeared in *Arc*, *Carousel*, *CV2*, *Event*, *The Fieldstone Review*, *FreeFall*, *The Malahat Review*, *Other Voices*, *The Prairie Journal*, *Room*, *subTerrain*, as well as with the Toronto Poetry Vendors and in the anthologies *Poems from Planet Earth* (Leaf Press) and *Best Canadian Poetry 2012* (Tightrope Books).

Laurie D Graham grew up in Sherwood Park, Alberta, and now lives in London, Ontario, where she is a poet, teacher, and editor of *Brick, A Literary Journal.* Her poems have appeared in numerous Canadian journals and anthologies, including *Event, Arc, The Malahat Review,* and *Best Canadian Poetry 2012.*